FIFTY FLUTE SOLOS

Arranged and edited by
John Sands.

Wise Publications
London/New York/Paris/Sydney/Copenhagen/Madrid

Exclusive Distributors:
Music Sales Limited
8/9 Frith Street, London W1V 5TZ, England.
Music Sales Pty Limited
120 Rothschild Avenue, Rosebery, NSW 2018, Australia.

ISBN 0-7119-1739-6
Order No. AM73289

Designed by Pearce Marchbank Studio
Compiled and arranged by John Sands

Printed in the United Kingdom by
J.B. Offset Printers (Marks Tey) Limited, Marks Tey, Essex.

TOUCH ME (I Want Your Body)

Words & Music by Jon Astrop, Mark Shreeve & Peter Harris.

Keep a steady tempo and observe the slurs.

I KNOW WHERE I'M GOIN'

Words & Music by Herbert Hughes.

Observe the key signature and give every note its full value.

LITTLE BROWN JUG

Traditional.

Repeat this one many times until the variations are at the same speed as the melody.

EIGHT DAYS A WEEK

Words & Music by John Lennon & Paul McCartney.

Make the tonguing crisp on the second variation and keep the tempo steady.

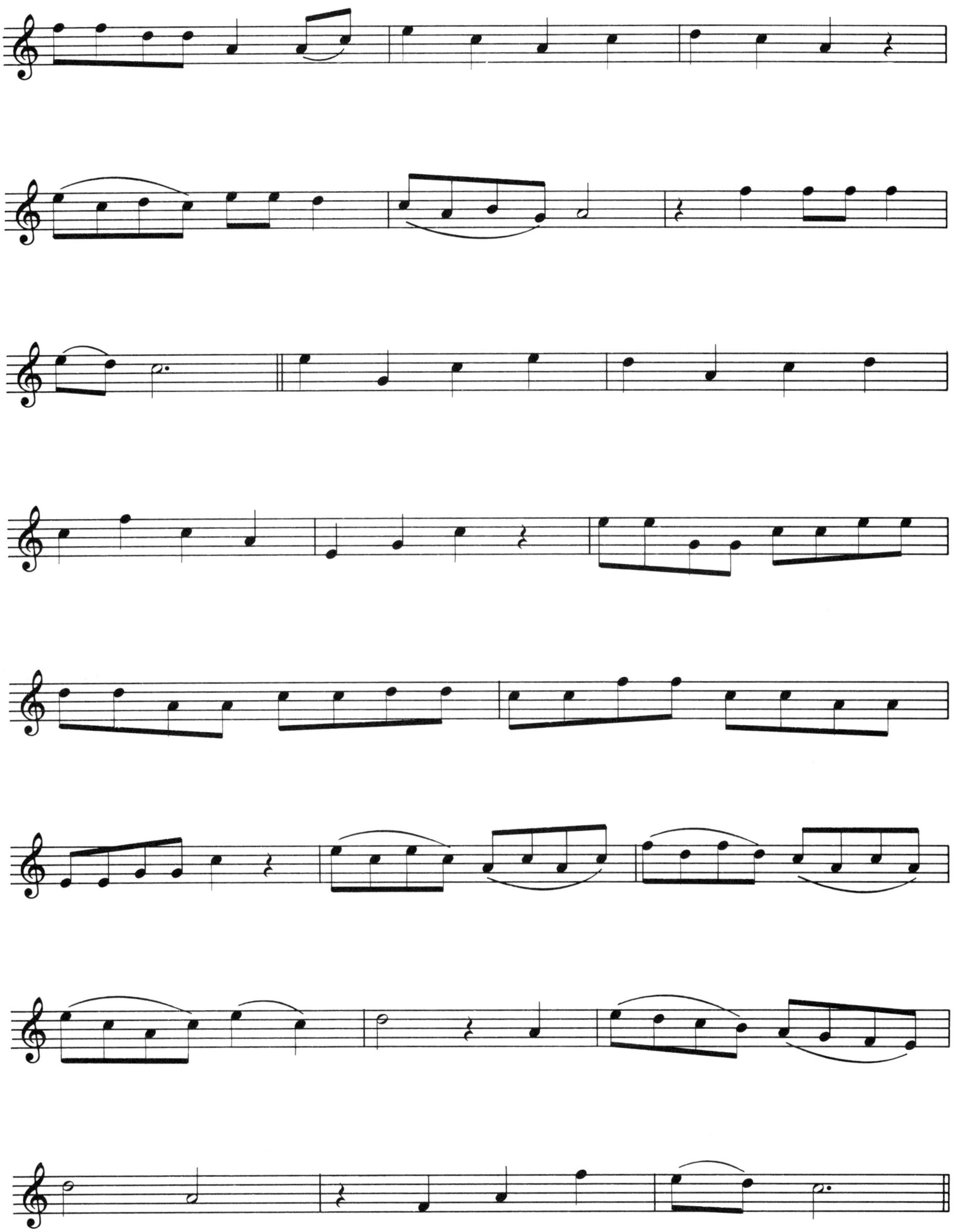

SUMMERTIME BLUES

Words & Music by Eddie Cochran & Jerry Capehart.

Keep the fingers close to the keys and check that the first finger of your left hand is raised when you play fourth line D.

ALL JOIN HANDS

Words & Music by Neville Holder & James Lea.

Accent the first beat in each bar and you will feel like dancing to this lovely song.

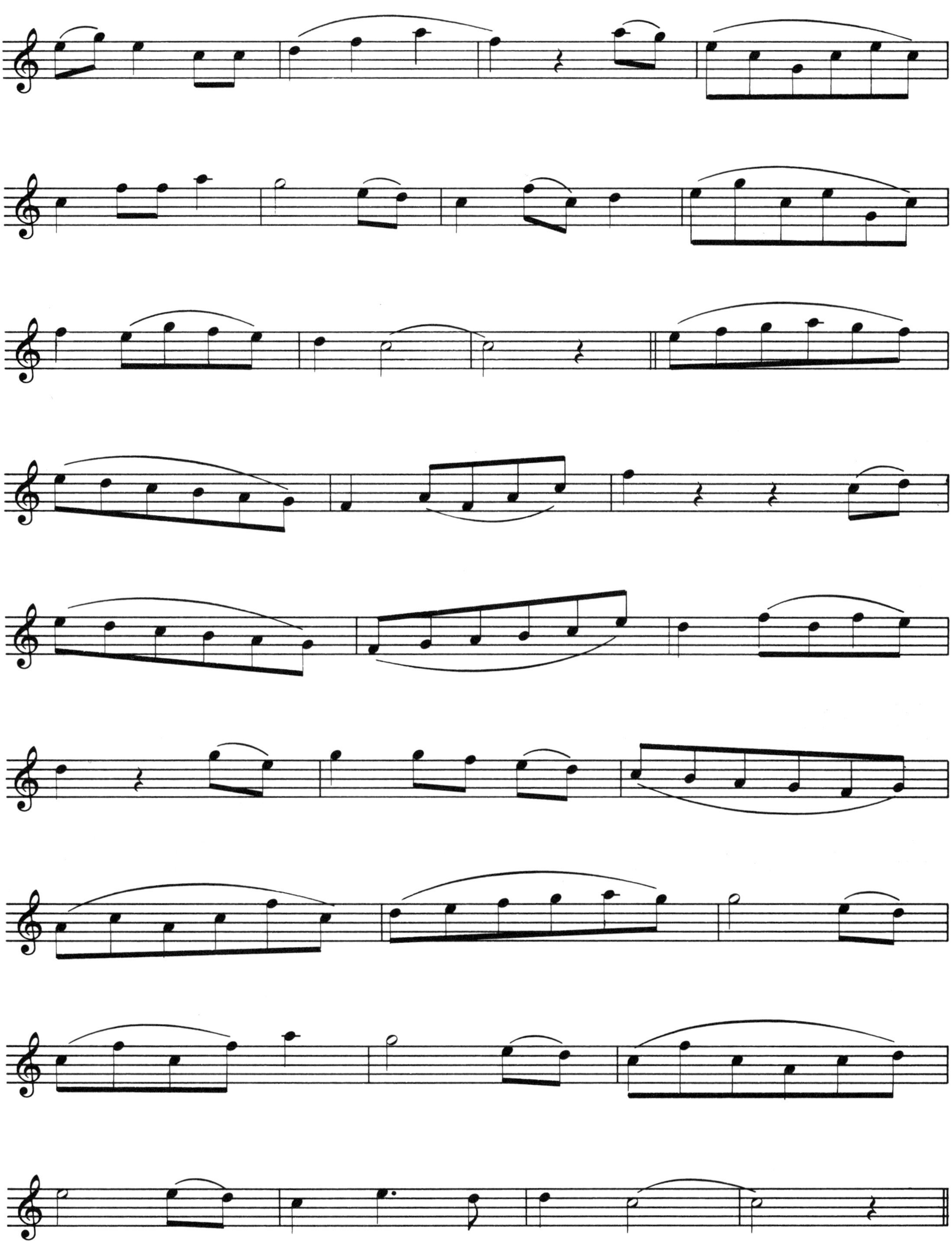

THE LITTLE SANDMAN

Composed by Johannes Brahms.

This famous classical tune should be played with a full tone and a steady pulse. Try to hear the tune in your head as you play the variation.

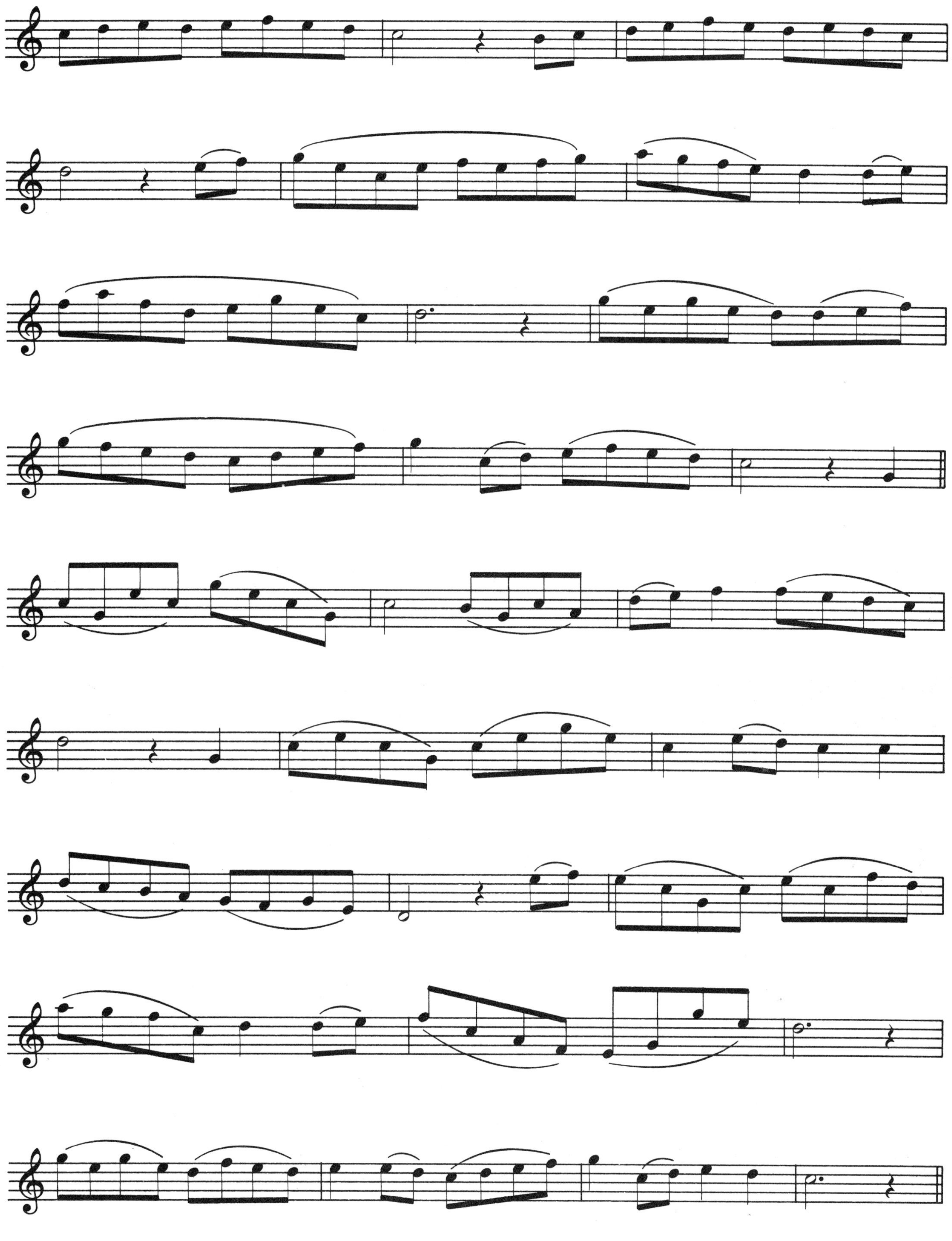

SUNNY

Words & Music by Bobby Hebb.

Lots of practise on the chords in the first variation will help to get your fingers 'moving'. Watch for 'enharmonic' notes D♭ (C♯), A♭ (G♯) and G♭ (F♯).

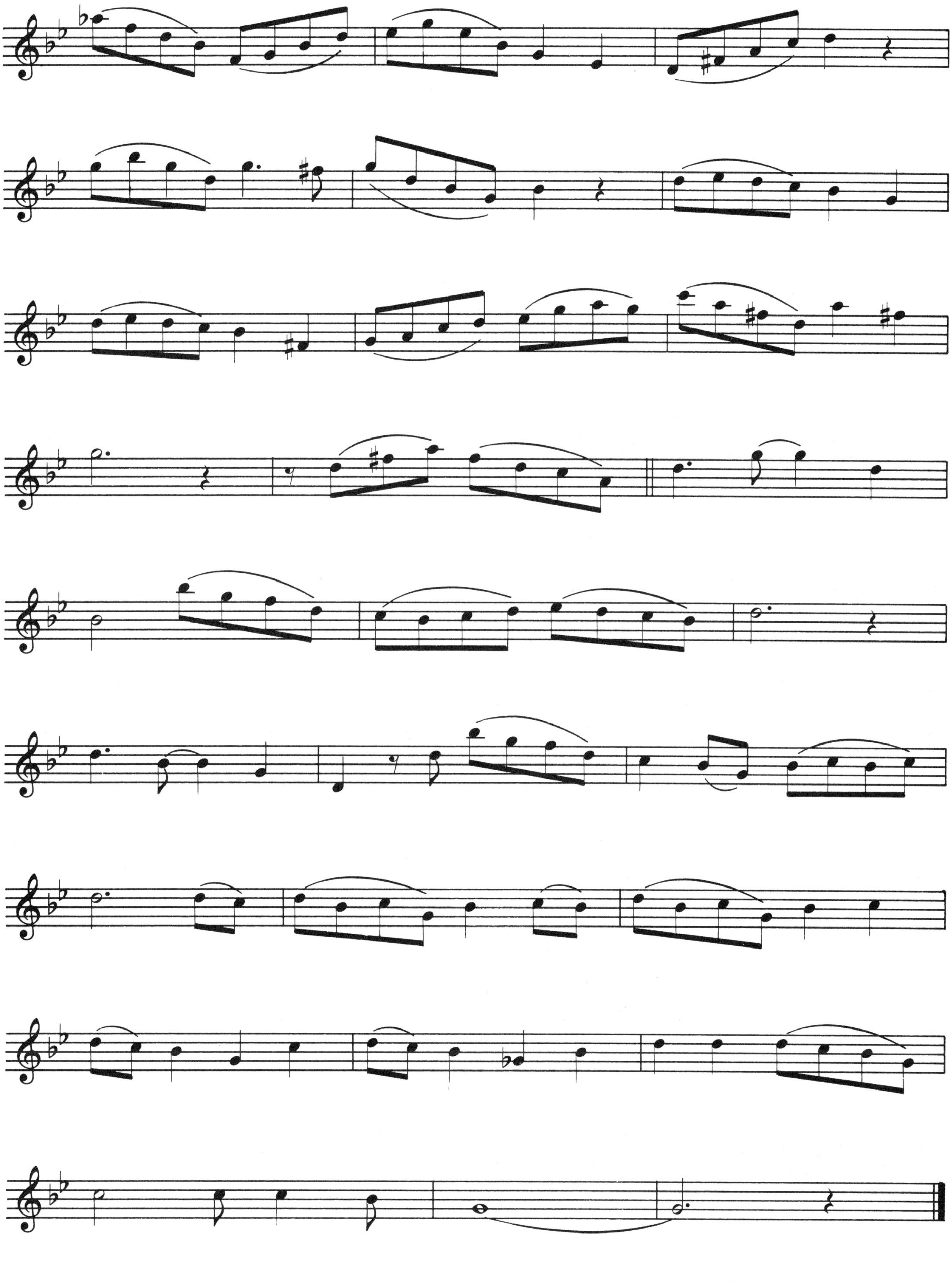

MR TAMBOURINE MAN

Words & Music by Bob Dylan.

Neat finger work in the first variation and crisp tonguing in the second will bring this famous song to life.

BLUE EYES CRYING IN THE RAIN

Words & Music by Fred Rose.

Observe the key signature in this well-known tune, but watch for the occasional accidental.

BLOWIN' IN THE WIND

Words & Music by Bob Dylan.

More practise in the key of A Major and some good chord practise in the last section.

BUFFALO SOLDIER

Words & Music by Bob Marley & Noel Williams.

The variations on this tune use the scale and chord of A Major.
Why not practise them from the scale and chord page
in The Complete Flute Player Book 1?

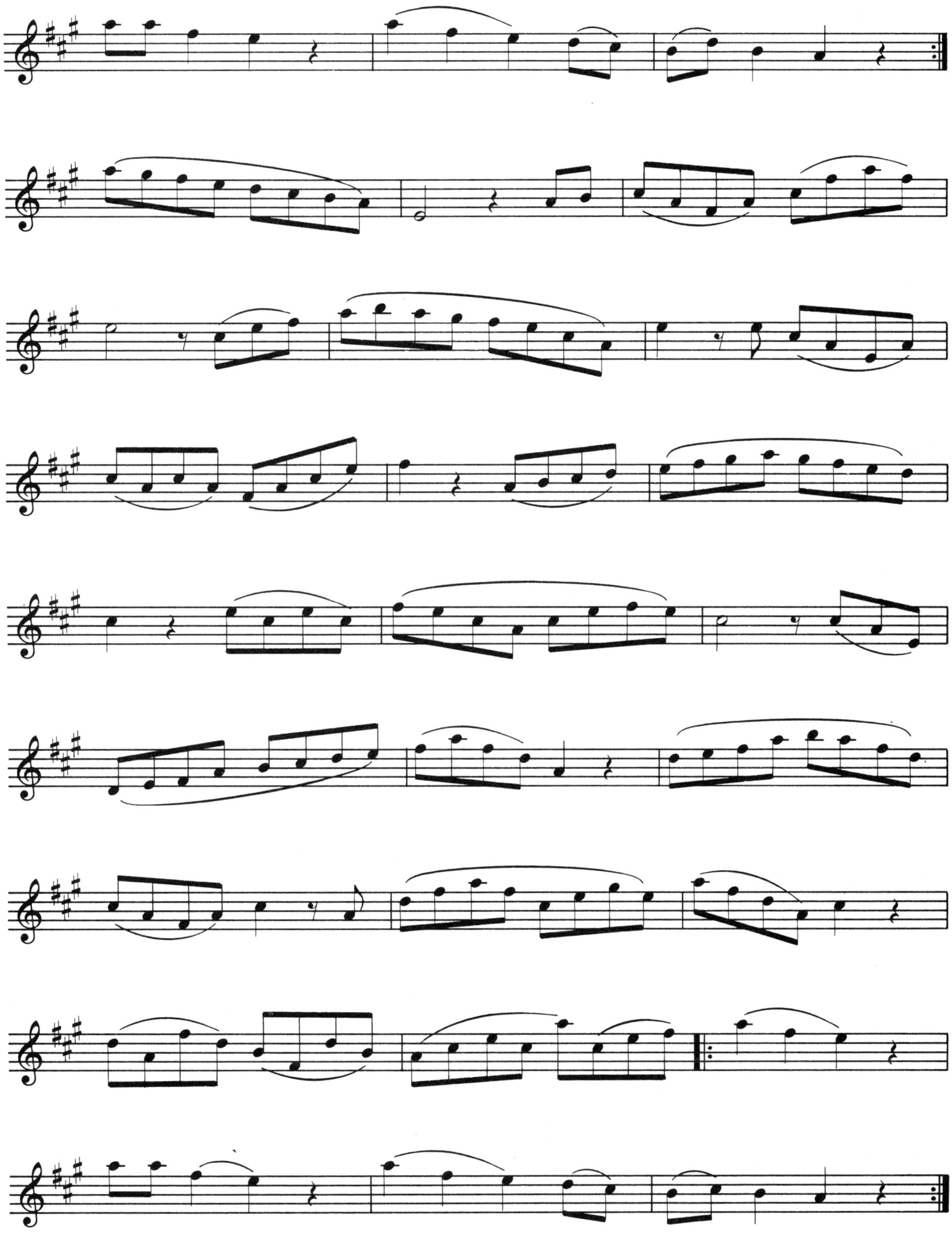

GATHERING APPLES

Traditional.

This traditional tune can be played at various speeds, but always observe the tongues and slurs.

BLACKBIRD

Words & Music by John Lennon & Paul McCartney.

This famous Beatles tune has some nice chord and scale runs.
Keep them smooth and 'song-like'.

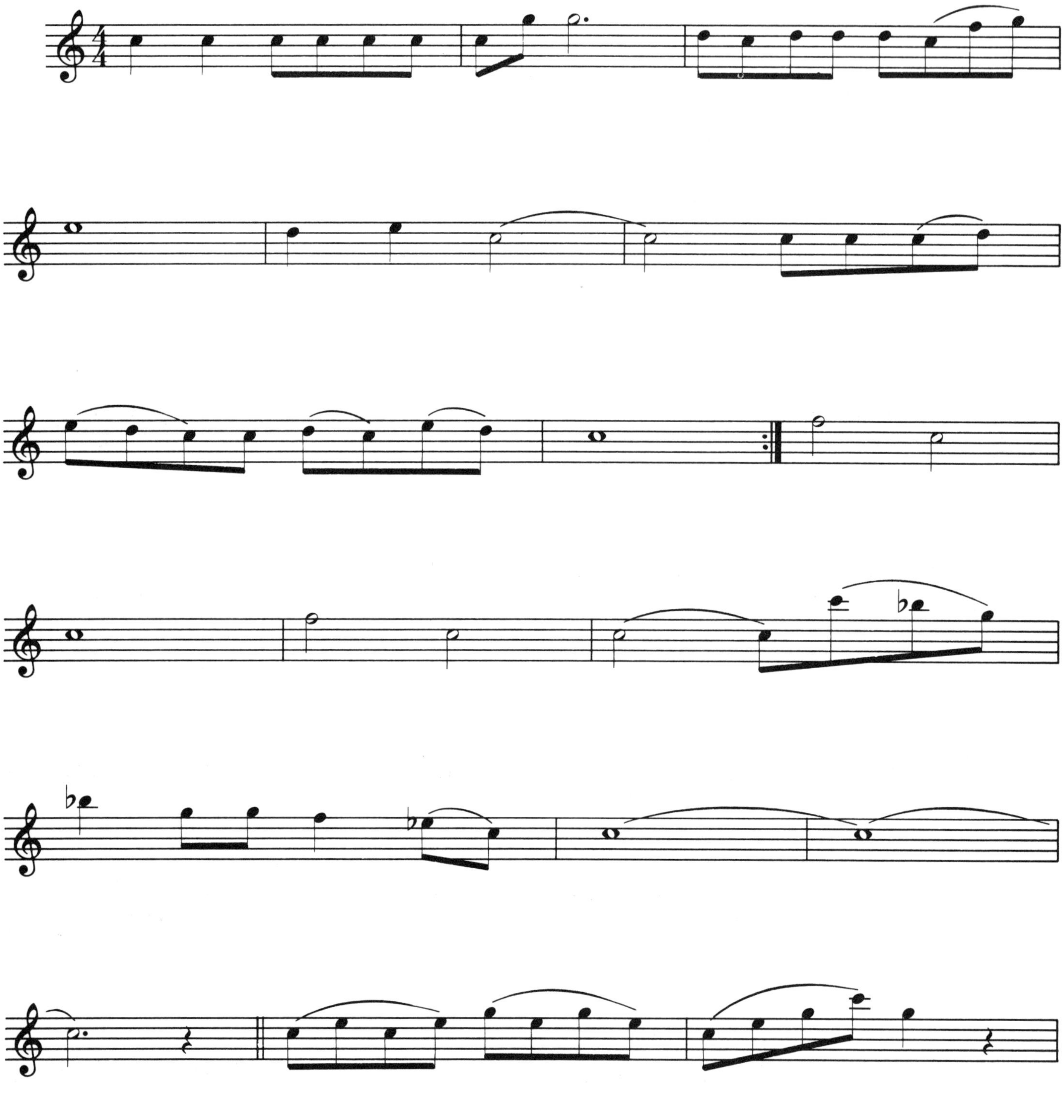

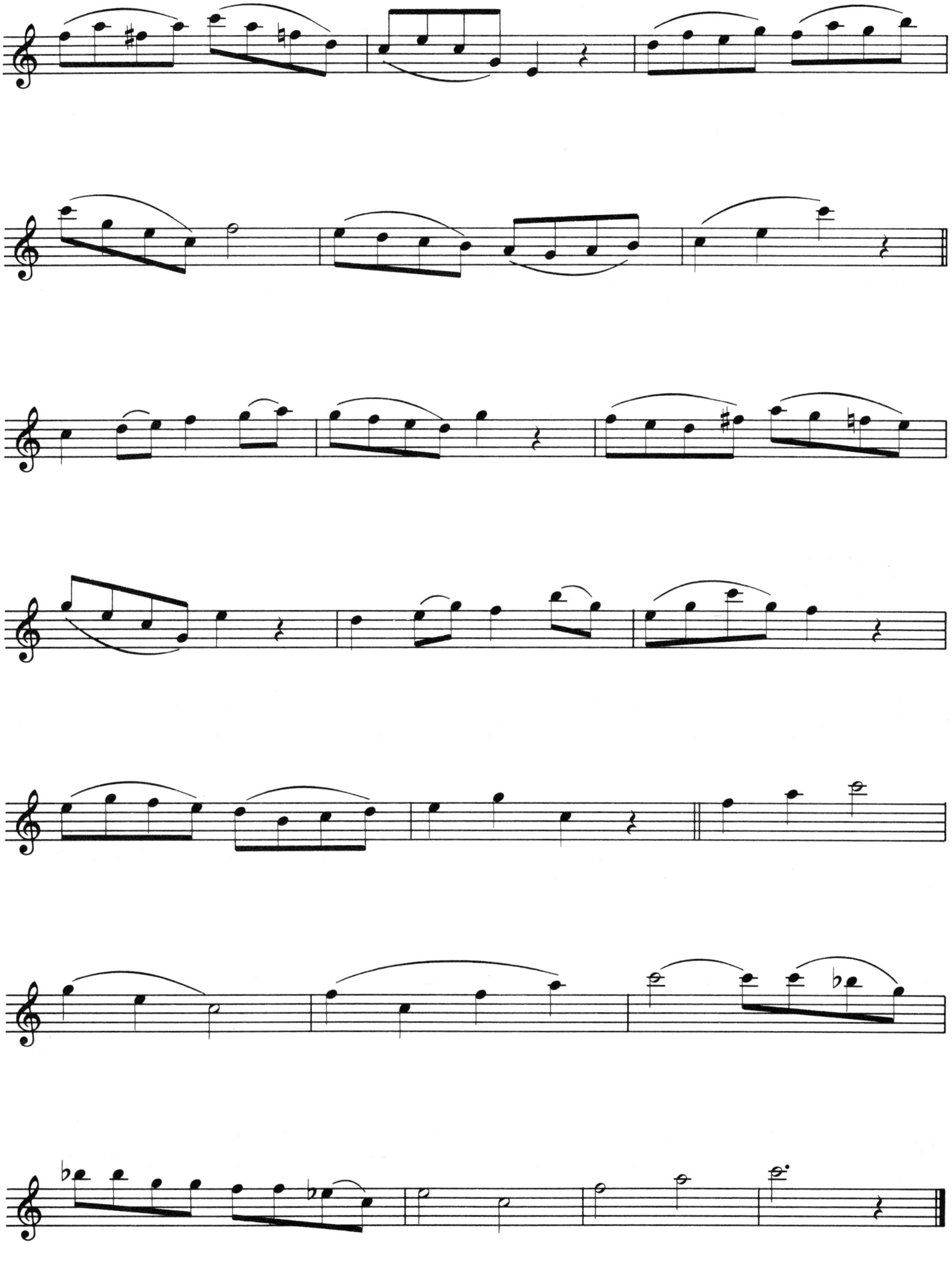

LOVE IS BLUE (L'Amour Est Bleu)

Music by André Popp.
Original Words by Pierre Cour.
English Lyric by Bryan Blackburn.

Look out for the change of key in this song and play with a pure singing tone.

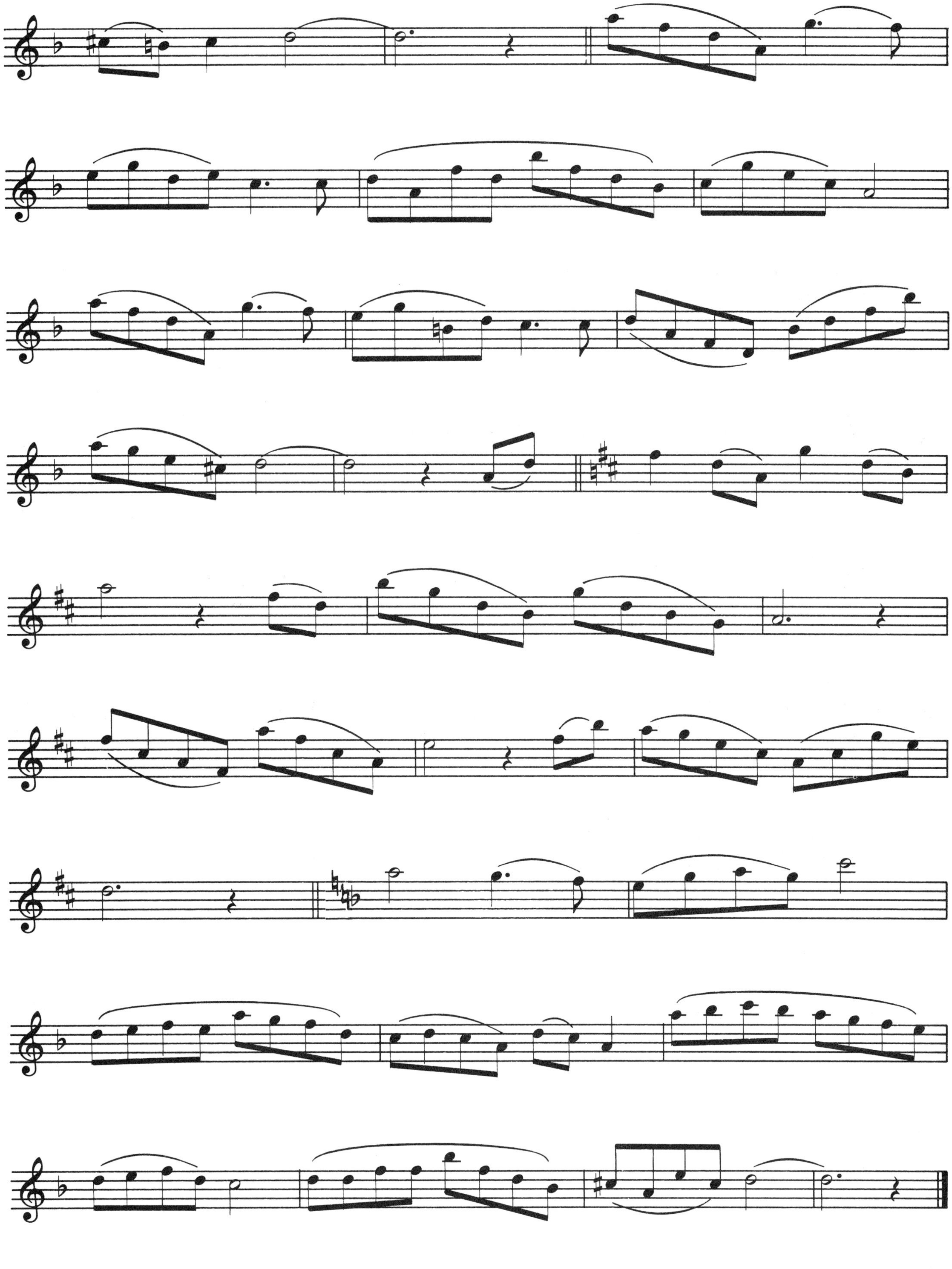

OH JULIE

Words & Music by Shakin' Stevens.

Keep a steady tempo throughout this piece, counting the rests carefully.
Tongue the crotchets in the variation, but let them have their full value.

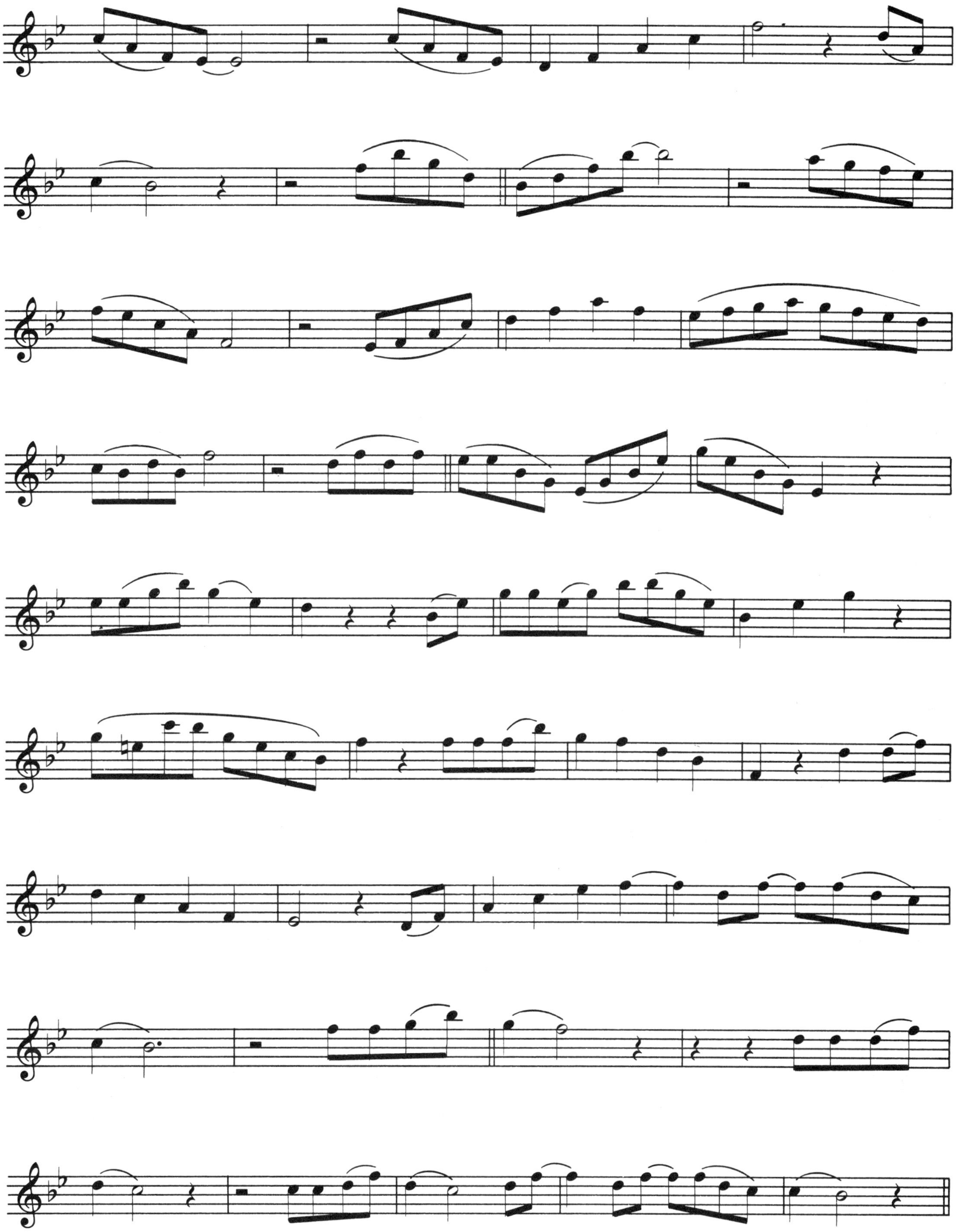

THE WINDMILLS OF YOUR MIND

Words by Alan & Marilyn Bergman.
Music by Michel Legrand.

Play this study using a soft tongue on the repeated notes.

MEMORIES OF YOU

Words by Andy Razaf.
Music by Eubie Blake.

This lovely old melody makes a good tone study. The tone should be vibrant and of equal quality from the lowest to the highest note.

LAZYBONES

Words & Music by Johnny Mercer & Hoagy Carmichael.

This study in dotted eighth notes also contains some difficult passages with accidentals in the variation. Practise each bar until you can play the whole piece smoothly and evenly.

LITTLE APRIL SHOWER

Words by Larry Morey.
Music by Frank Churchill.

The variations on this tune are mainly rhythmic. Keep a steady pulse throughout and slightly accent the 'off beat' notes.

BESAME MUCHO

English Words by Sunny Skylar.
Music by Consuelo Velazquez.

Practise this Latin American tune with a pure singing tone. Make the scale runs on the variation smooth and even. The key is D Minor.

SHE LOVES YOU

Words & Music by John Lennon & Paul McCartney.

Play this smoothly and quietly and look out for the accidentals in the variation.

1.
2.

I'VE GOT NO STRINGS

Words by Ned Washington.
Music by Leigh Harline.

Practise the A Major scale from the scale page of The Complete Flute Player Book 2 and you will find the benefit when you play the variations on this lively tune.

WORLD WITHOUT LOVE

Words & Music by John Lennon & Paul McCartney.

Another lovely song from the pen of Lennon and McCartney.
Play it smoothly with an elegant style and pure tone.

1.
2.

THE BALLAD OF DAVY CROCKETT

Words by Tom Blackburn.
Music by George Bruns.

Keep the fingers close to the keys in the passages using high E and do not blow hard. Check back to The Complete Flute Player Book 2 Lesson 7 for the best way to play this note.

IRISH WASHERWOMAN

Traditional.

Lots of fun to be had playing this traditional tune in $\frac{6}{8}$. Practise until the finger and tongue work is as one, then there is no limit to the speed it can be played.

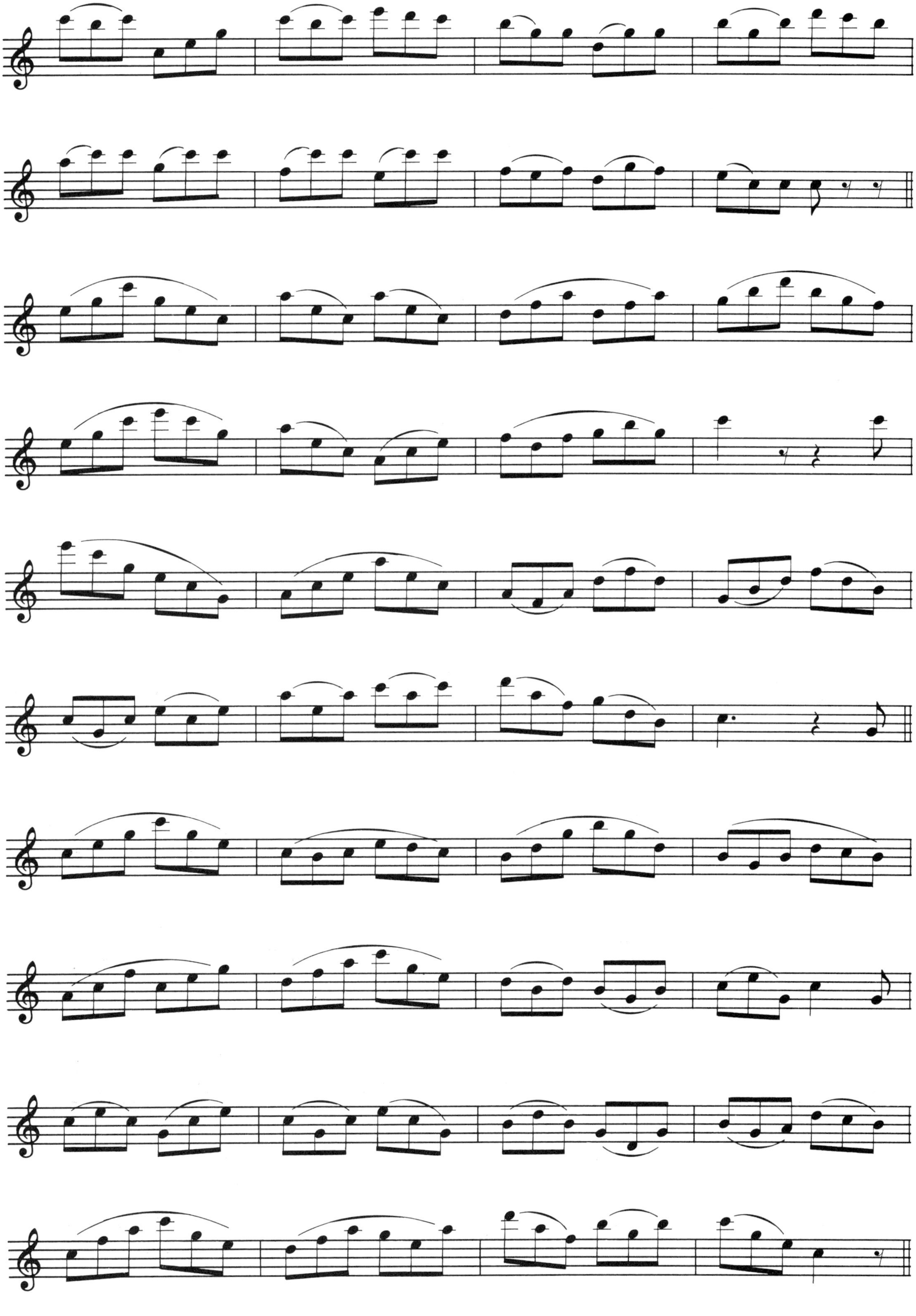

MARCH OF THE GRENADIERS

Words by Clifford Grey. Additional Words by Reg Connelly.
Music by Victor Schertzinger.

Another chance to play in $\frac{6}{8}$ time, here in a march. Do not play too quickly as there are some 'tricky' runs in the variation.

HEIGH HO

Words & Music by Larry Morey & Frank Churchill.

Another chance to play high F and lots of scale passages in this lively song.

THE BARE NECESSITIES

Words & Music by Terry Gilkyson.

Practise the chords in this variation until you can play them smoothly and evenly, and check your fingering for top F in the variation.

NELLIE THE ELEPHANT

Words by Ralph Butler.
Music by Peter Hart.

Neat finger work is needed for this fun tune. Look out for the change of key and take note that the variation comes before the tune in the new key.

GIVE A LITTLE WHISTLE

Words by Ned Washington.
Music by Leigh Harline.

This song should be played lightly with the repeated notes in the melody clearly articulated. Lots of E Major scale practise would smooth the way for the variation

WHISTLE WHILE YOU WORK

Words & Music by Larry Morey & Frank Churchill.

The scale runs in the variation must be practised slowly until they are smooth and even, then try to match them to the speed of the melody.

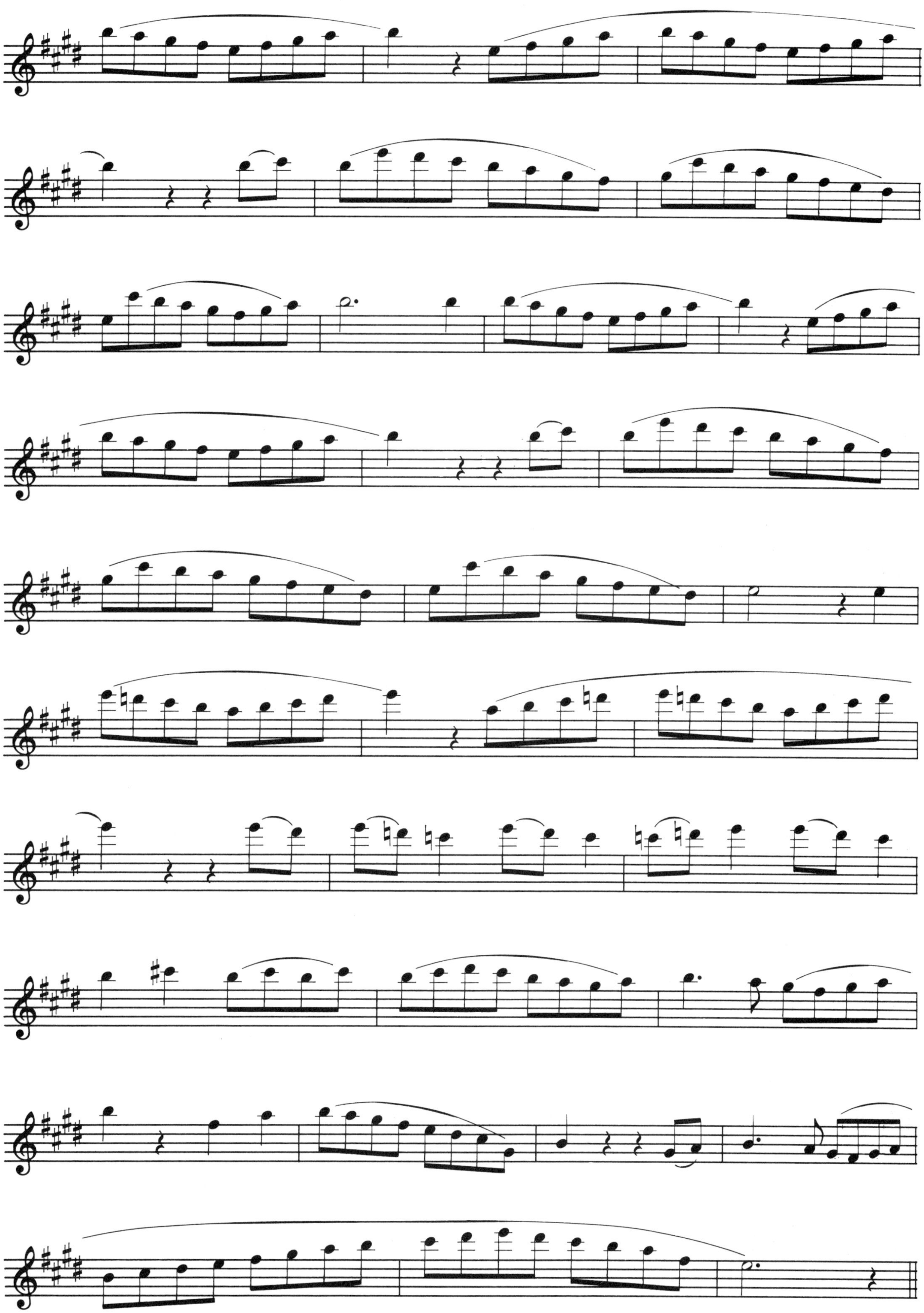

MELODY IN F

Composed by Anton Rubinstein.

Practise this haunting melody with a loose lip and jaw, and make the tone vibrant. Low C♯ and C♮ are not the easiest notes to play on the flute, they need a good supply of air, so use the lower part of your lungs as described in The Complete Flute Player Book 1.

LAVENDER BLUE

Traditional.

The variation provides a good opportunity to practise triplets and good tonguing practise when you come to the section with the dotted eighth notes.

WHEN YOU WISH UPON A STAR

Words by Ned Washington.
Music by Leigh Harline.

The variation on this beautiful melody is a study in ascending and descending octaves. Try to keep the shape of the melody throughout.

ALL THE THINGS YOU ARE

Music by Jerome Kern.
Words by Oscar Hammerstein II.

Another chance to play in alla breve time and some good chord practice in the variation.

3
(♭)
3

LOVE AND MARRIAGE

Words by Sammy Cahn.
Music by James Van Heusen.

Play this study rather slowly, making the scales in the variation even and smooth. Do not blow hard for the top notes.

SPINNING WHEEL

Words & Music by David Clayton Thomas.

A steady rhythm is needed in this song to get maximum effect.

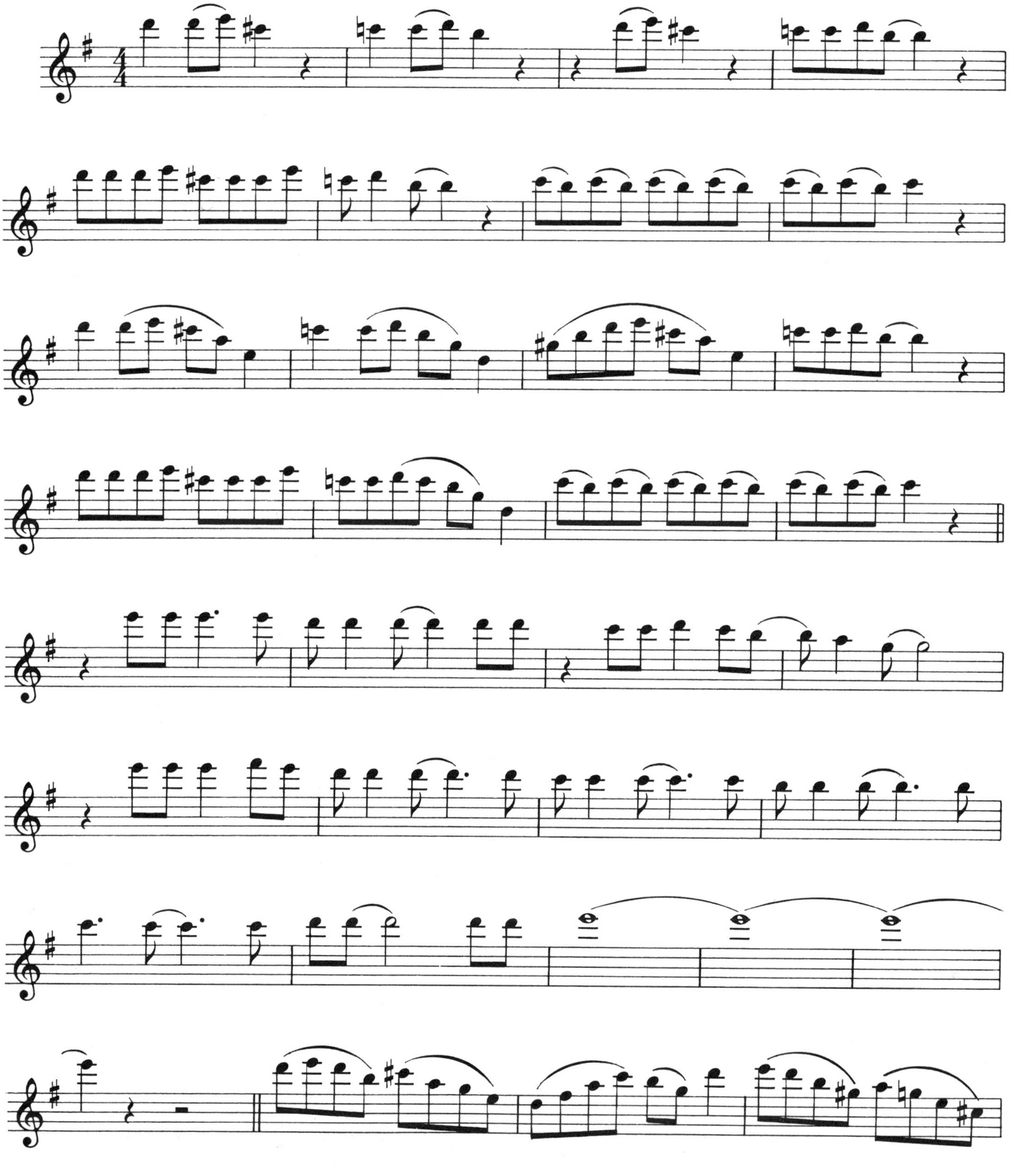

BILL BAILEY WON'T YOU PLEASE COME HOME

Traditional.

Neat fingering on the chromatic scale runs will help you to get this traditional tune up to tempo.

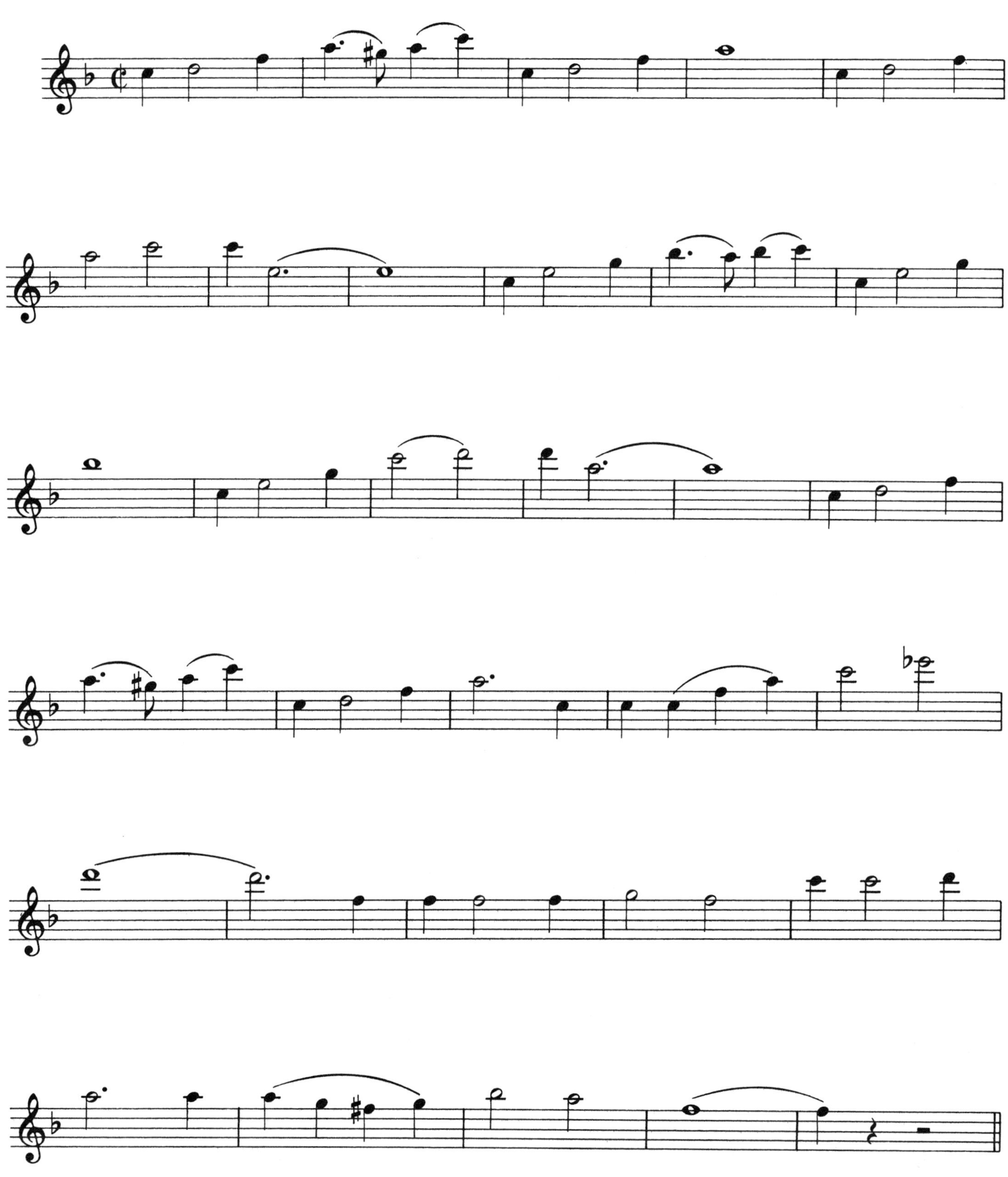

IN A SENTIMENTAL MOOD

Words & Music by Duke Ellington, Irving Mills & Manny Kurtz.

Observe the dynamics in this tune and keep a steady rhythm throughout.

THE INCH WORM

Words & Music by Frank Loesser.

The scale passages in the variation of this song must be smooth and even.

I'M IN A DANCING MOOD

Words & Music by Maurice Sigler, Al Goodhart & Al Hoffman.

Do not blow hard for the top notes in the variation. Keep a relaxed lip and make sure you have the correct fingering.

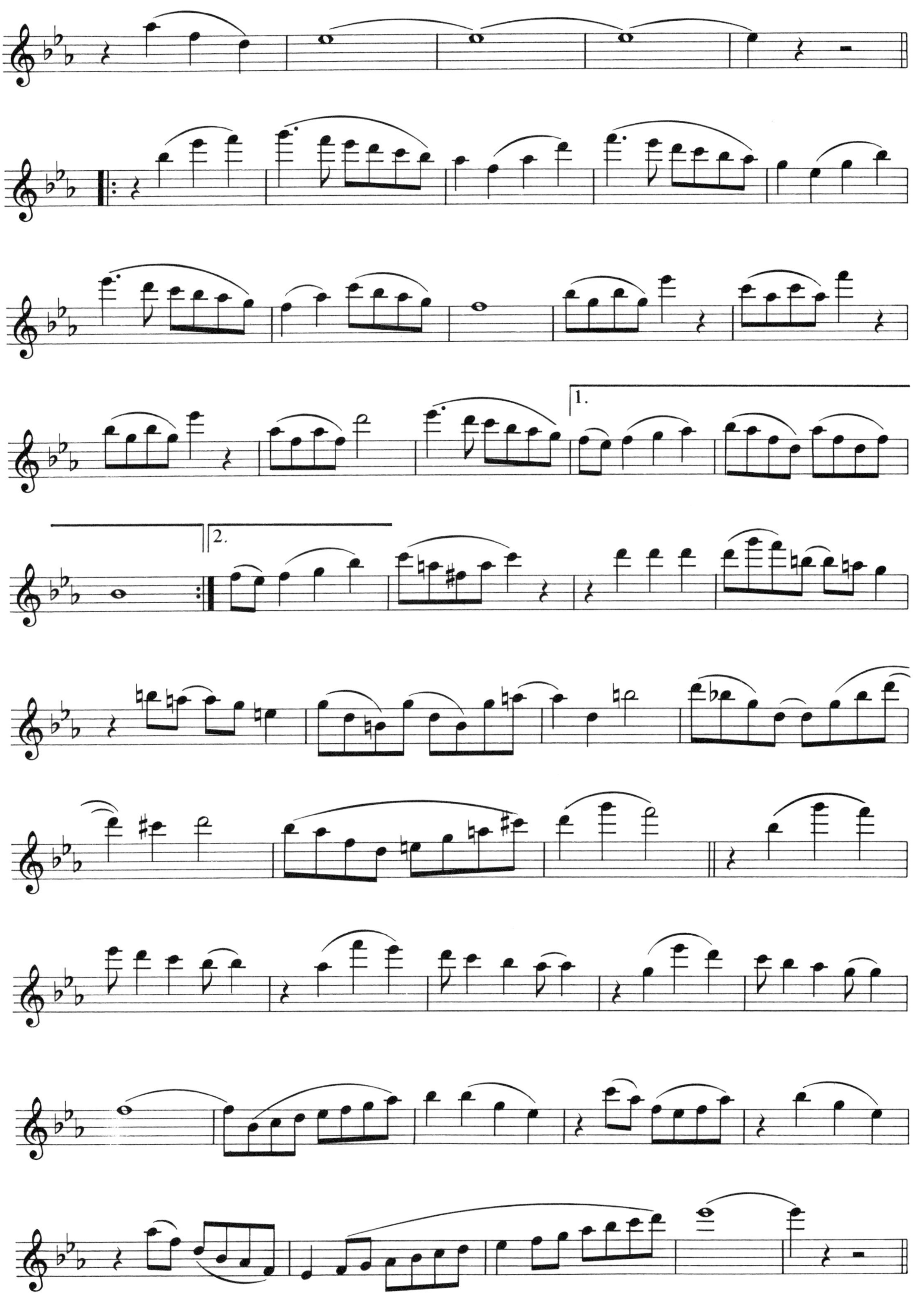
1.
2.

DIAMONDS ARE A GIRL'S BEST FRIEND

Words by Leo Robin.
Music by Jule Styne.

This study climbs gradually to high G♯ and A♮.

tr

FASCINATION

Music by F.D. Marchetti.
English Lyric by Dick Manning.

Practise your dynamics on this lovely melody. Observe the change of key in the middle section.

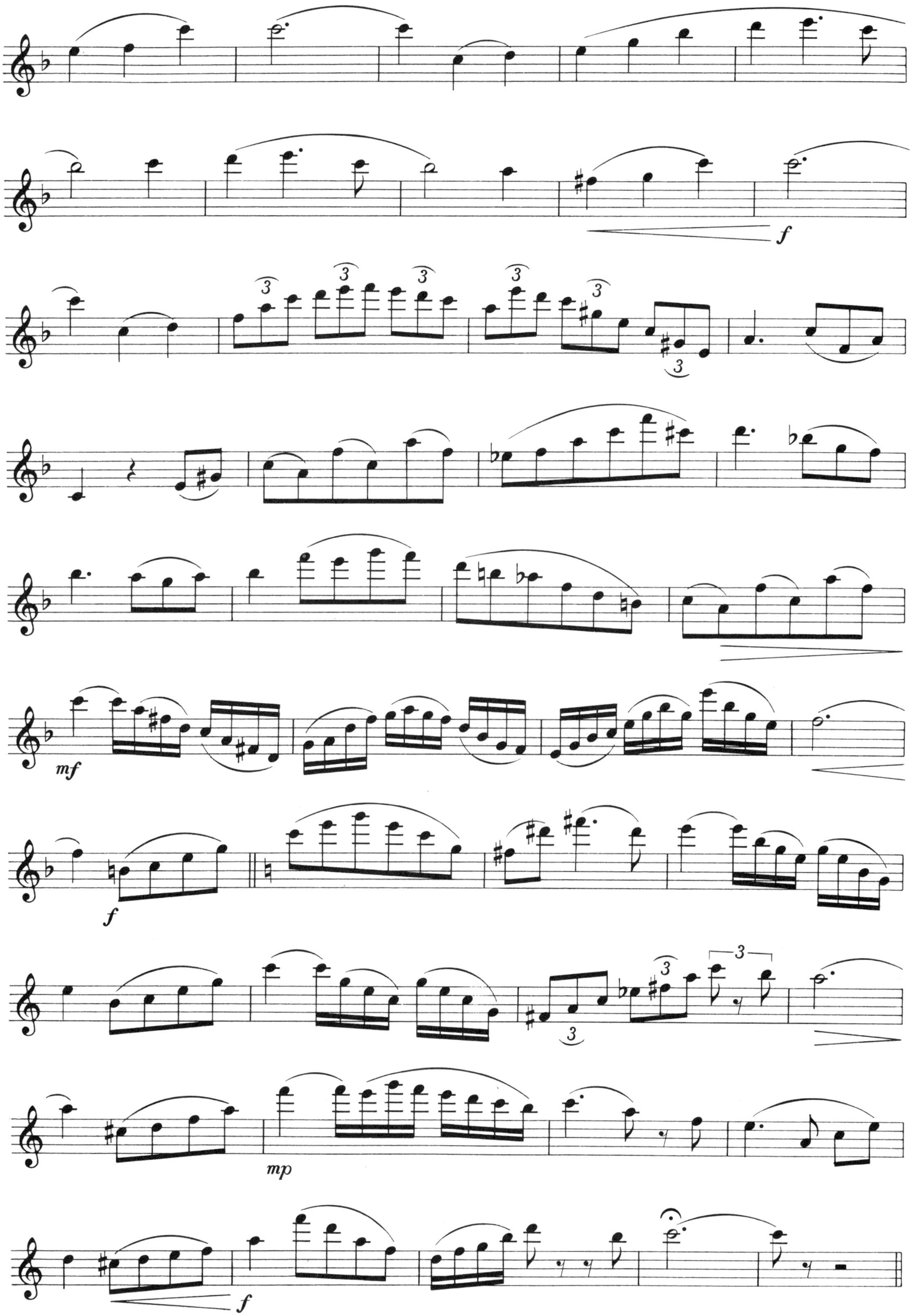
f
mf
f
mp
f

STARS FELL ON ALABAMA

Words by Mitchell Parish.
Music by Frank Perkins.

The chord of the diminished seventh is to be found in the variation on this melody.

mp
mf
f
p
f

UNDER THE BRIDGES OF PARIS
(Sous Les Ponts De Paris)

Music by Vincent Scotto.
French Lyric by J.Rodor. English Lyric by Dorcas Cochran.

Check that you have the correct fingering for the high B♭ (A♯) and practise the runs until they are smooth and even.

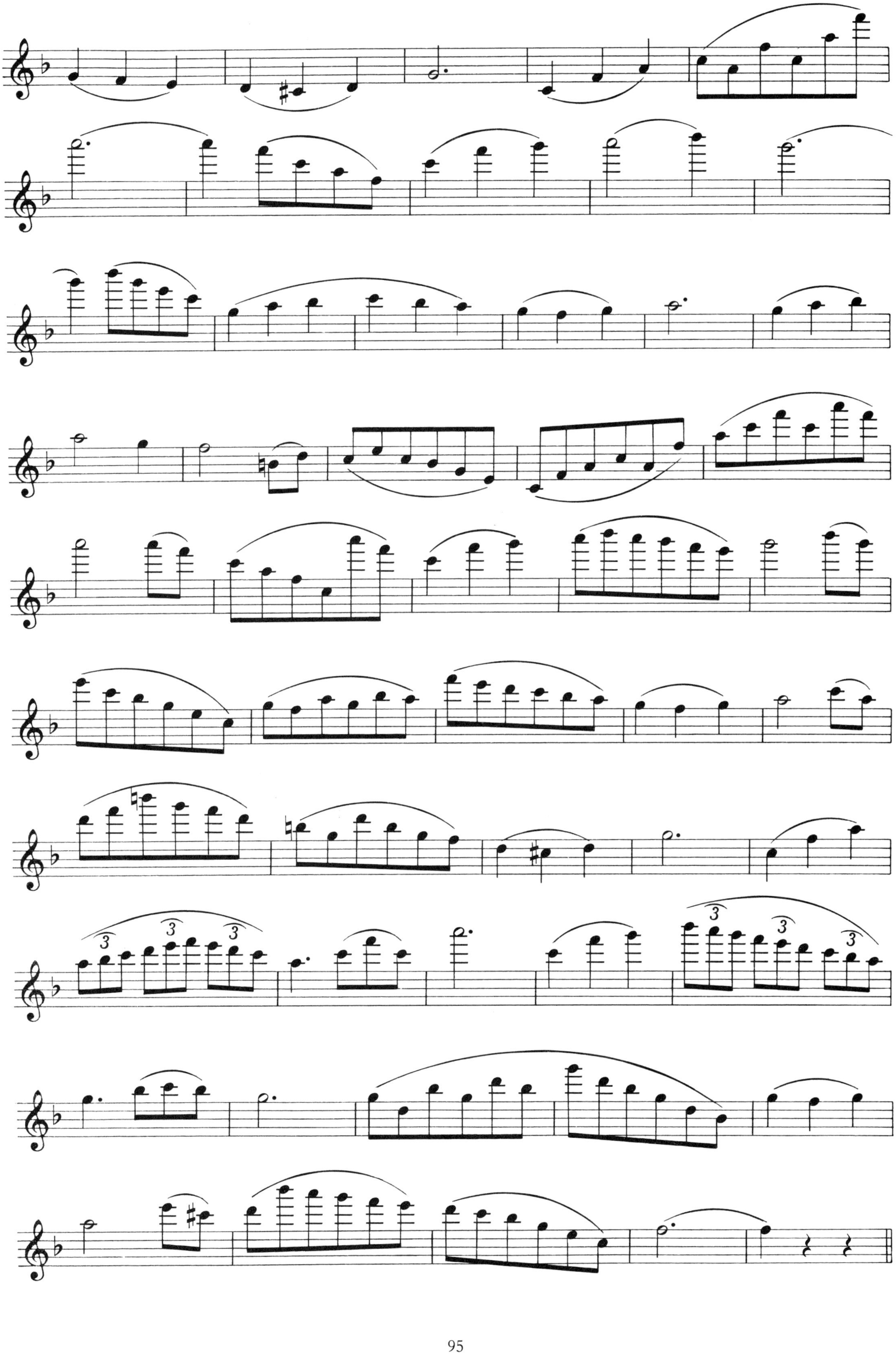

LULLABY OF BIRDLAND

Music by George Shearing.
Words by George David Weiss.

High B♮ comes only once in this piece. Have the correct fingering and do not overblow, use your changing lip technique.

3

TOP OF THE WORLD

Words by John Bettis.
Music by Richard Carpenter.

Careful tonguing and slurring in this study will create a smooth rhythmic effect.

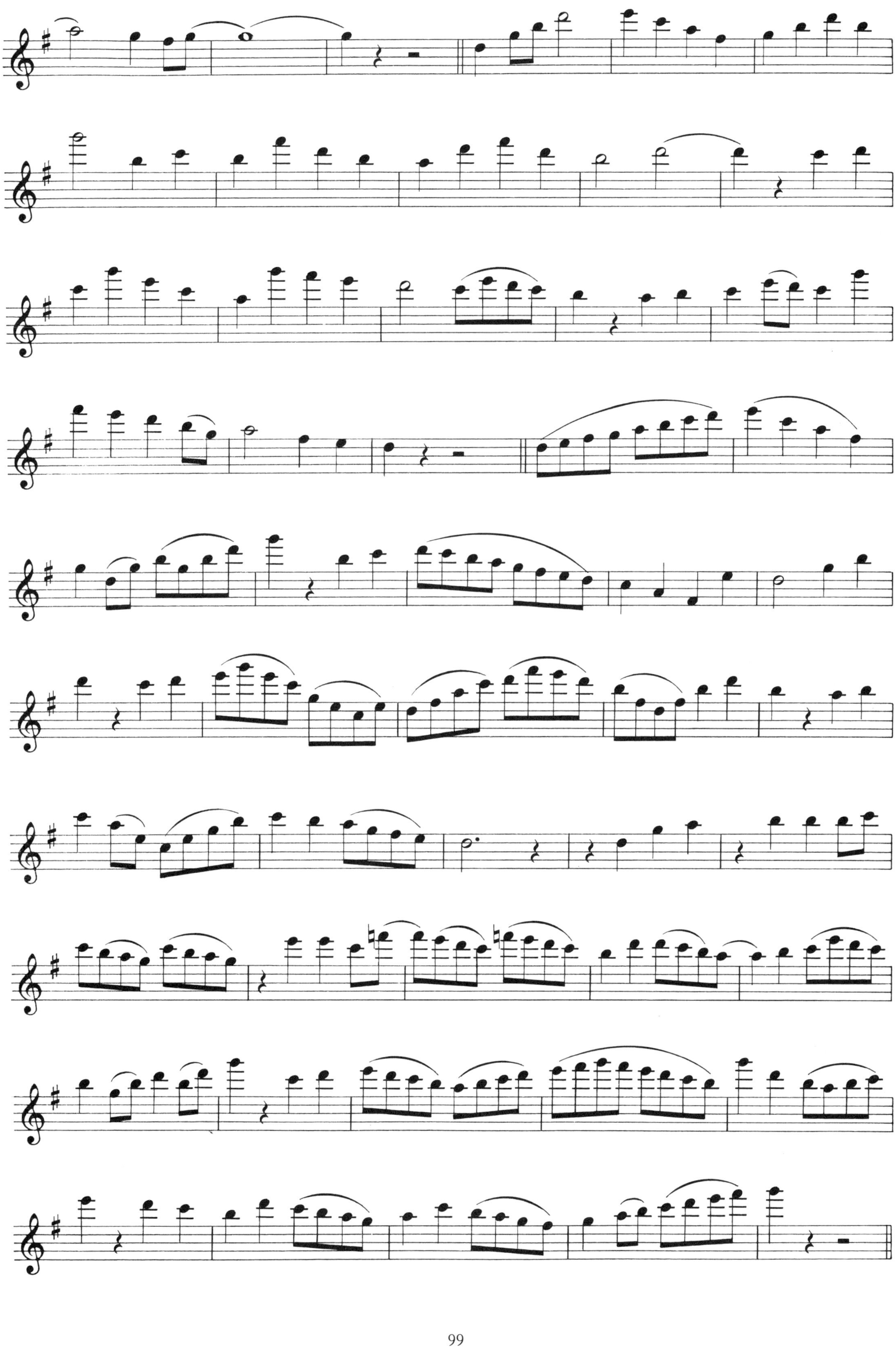

STARDUST

Words by Mitchell Parish.
Music by Hoagy Carmichael.

The variation is quite difficult, both rhythmically and technically, but time spent perfecting it will be worthwhile. When it is mastered you can truly say that you are well on the way to becoming 'the complete flute player'.

mp
f
mp
f

SAILING

Words & Music by Gavin Sutherland.

The variations on this song are mostly chordal. Keep them smooth and even.

The Beatles

Enya

Phil Collins

Van Morrison

Bob Dylan

Sting

Paul Simon

Tracy Chapman

Bringing you the words

Eric Clapton

Pink Floyd

New Kids On The Block

All the latest in rock and pop. Plus the brightest and best in West End show scores. Music books for every instrument under the sun. And exciting new teach-yourself ideas like "Let's Play Keyboard" - in cassette/book packs, or on video. Available from all good music shops.

Bryan Adams

Tina Turner

Elton John

Bee Gees

Whitney Houston

AC/DC

and music

Music Sales' complete catalogue lists thousands of titles and is available free from your local music shop, or direct from Music Sales Limited. Please send a cheque or postal order for £1.50 (for postage) to:

Music Sales Limited
Newmarket Road,
Bury St Edmunds,
Suffolk IP33 3YB

Buddy

Five Guys Named Moe

Les Misérables

West Side Story

Phantom Of The Opera

Show Boat

The Rocky Horror Show

Bringing you the world's best music.